1819

LA MAITRESSE DE BRODERIE
THE MISTRESS OF EMBROIDERY

PATTERNS FOR EMBROIDERY, COUNTED CROSS STITCH & NEEDLEPOINT

⊱ 1819 ⊰

La Maitresse de Broiderie

The Mistress of Embroidery

a quality digital reproduction of an antique book
full of charted designs, embroidery patterns and inspiration for modern needleworkers

by
Art of the Needle Publishing

© 2018 All Rights Reserved.
Reproduction by any means, including digital and print, is prohibited.

Questions? Comments? Write us at ArtoftheNeedlePublishing@gmail.com

Available in both print and ebook formats through Amazon.

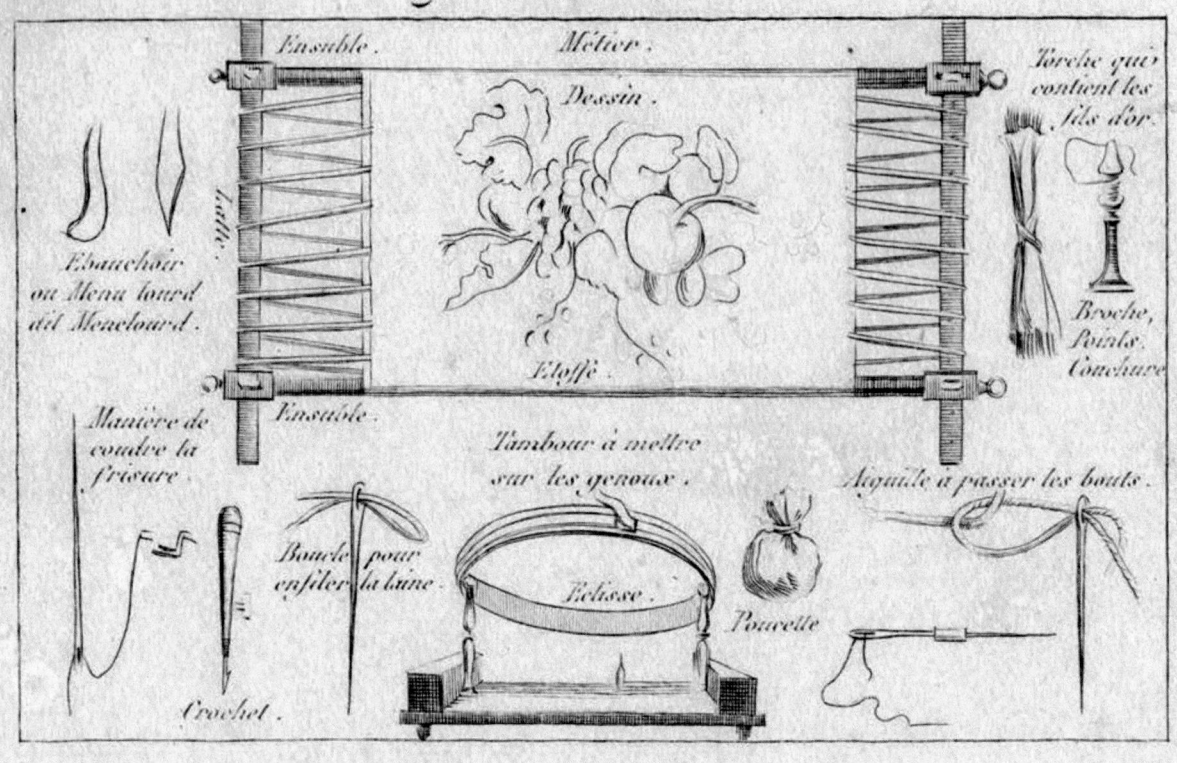

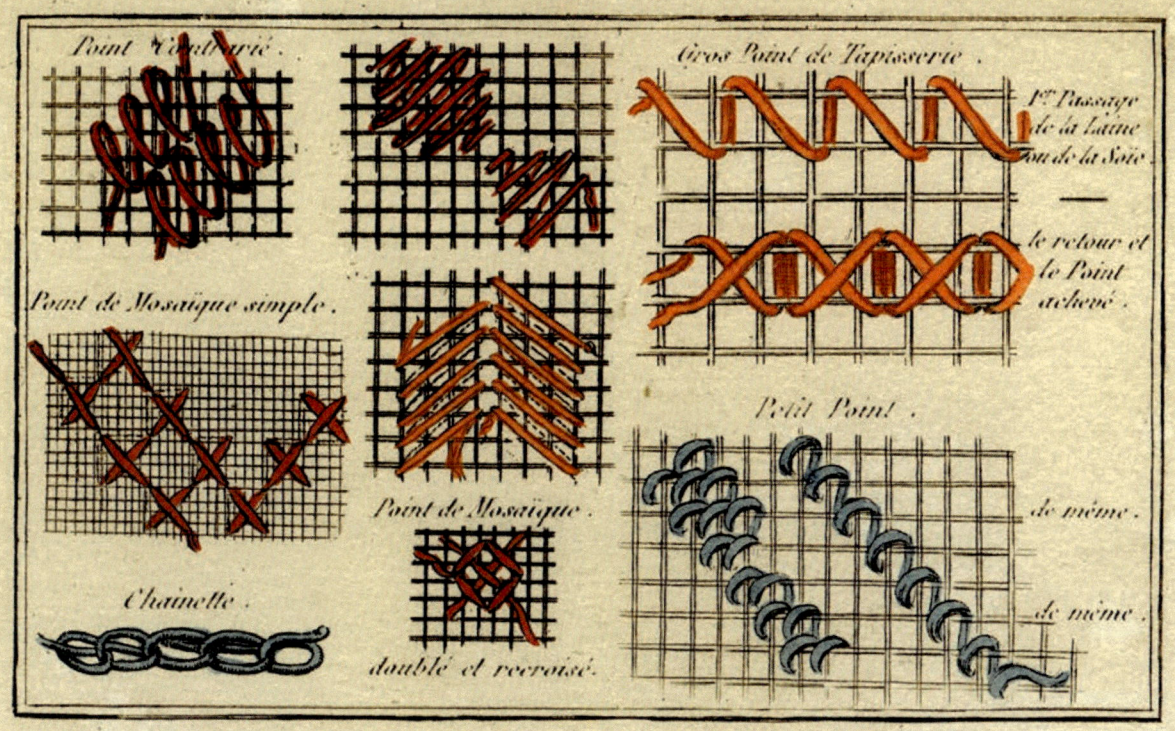

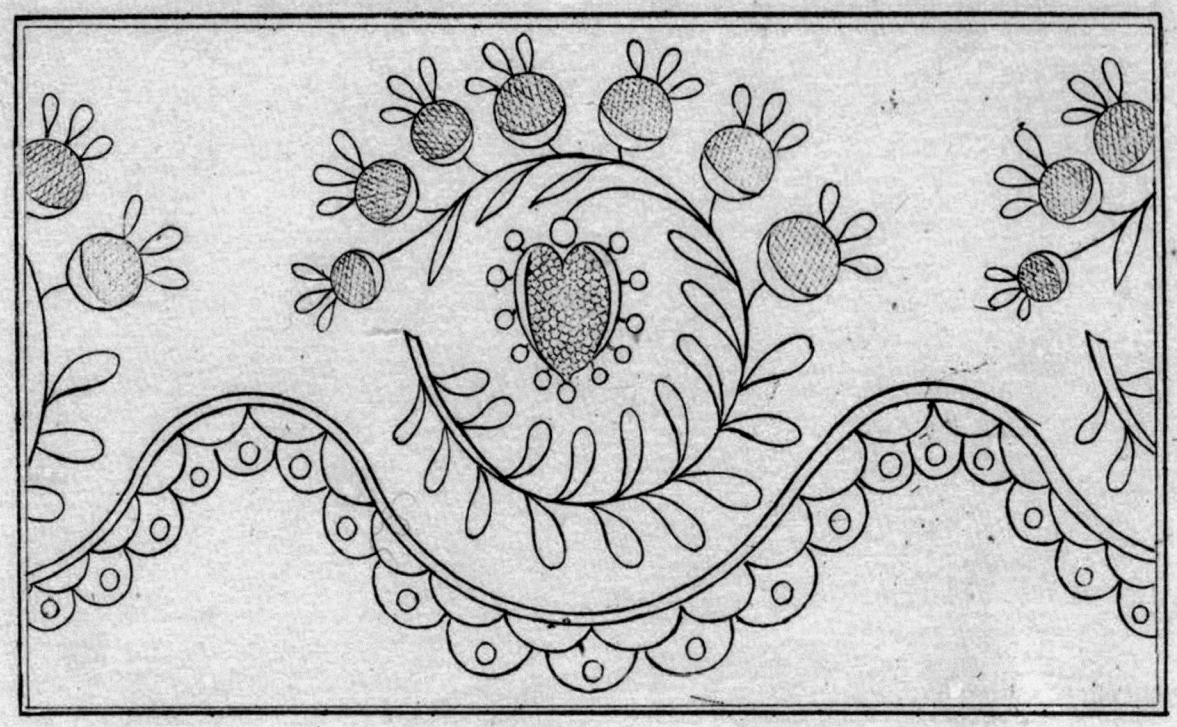

Broderie au Plumetis. F. 4.

THE MISTRESS OF EMBROIDERY PAGE 9

THE MISTRESS OF EMBROIDERY   PAGE 11

THE MISTRESS OF EMBROIDERY · PAGE 12

THE MISTRESS OF EMBROIDERY — PAGE 14

THE MISTRESS OF EMBROIDERY

Tapisserie, N° 15.

THE MISTRESS OF EMBROIDERY   PAGE 18

THE MISTRESS OF EMBROIDERY — PAGE 19

THE MISTRESS OF EMBROIDERY

Tapisserie, N°. 19.

Marque N°. de Suite 36.

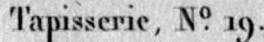

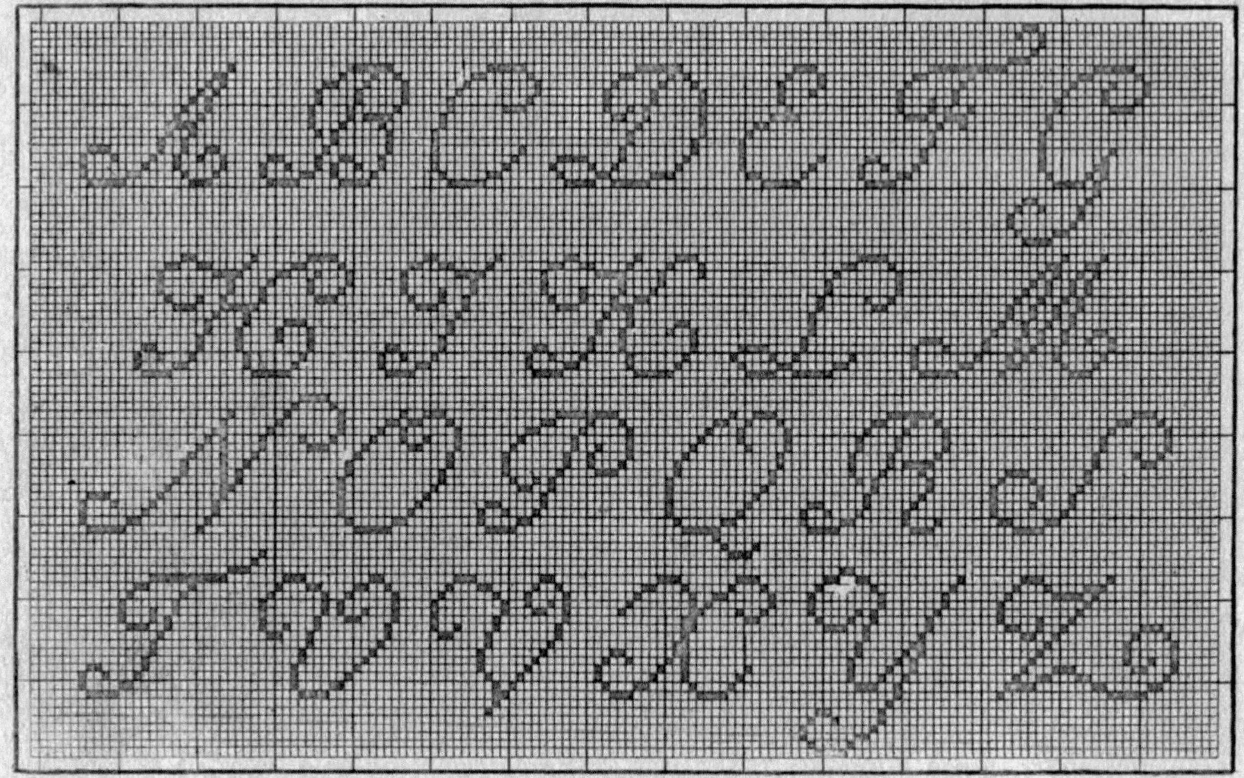

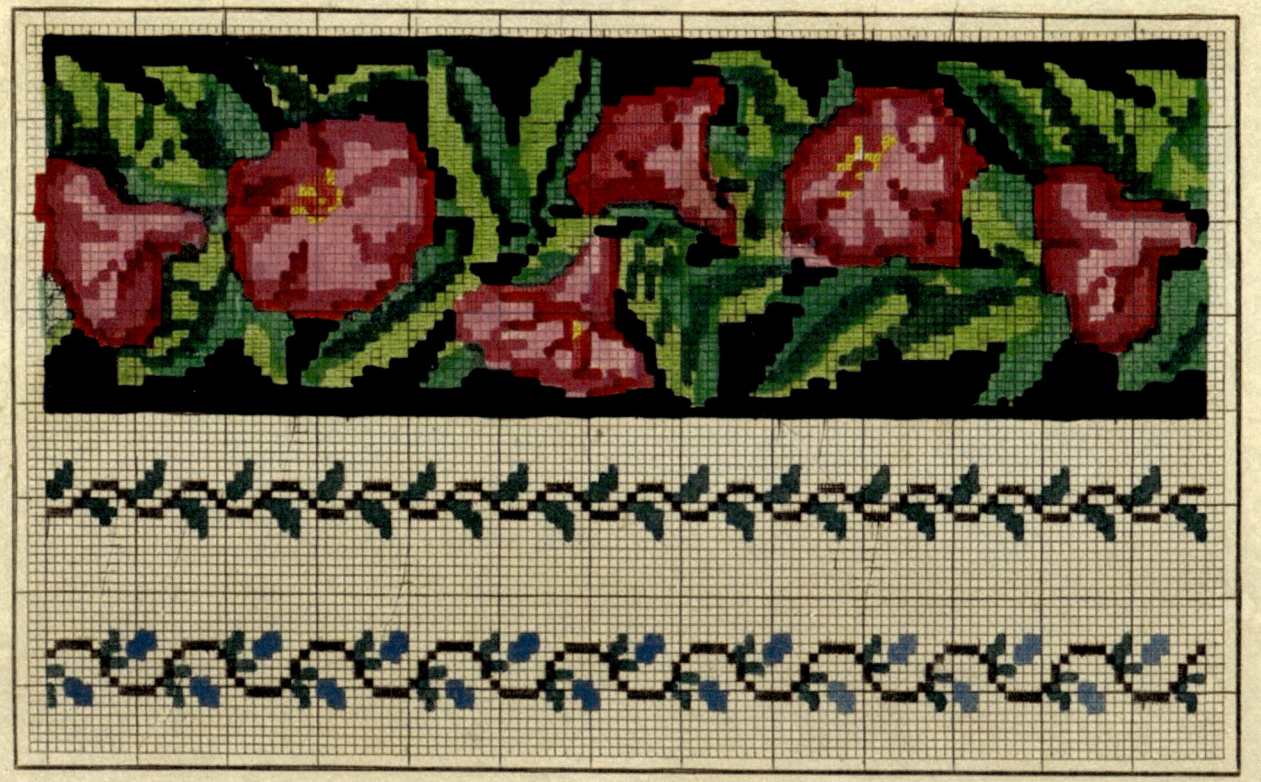

Broderie en Or. 21.

Tableau qui doit être Brodé d'Or nué.
a. Partie dessinée au Trait.
b. Les fils d'or qui ne sont que lancés.
c. Ceux qui sont recouverts de soie pour former les ombres.
d. Partie d'une figure qui est satinée en soie nuée tout d'un sens et sans or dessous.
Les cheveux se font en soie.

Fleur de Lys Gauffrée à moitié.
a. Fils lancés à deux lignes les uns des autres.
b. L'or cousu de deux fils en deux fils.
c. Le cordon qui lisère la Fleur.

Broderie en Or. 22.

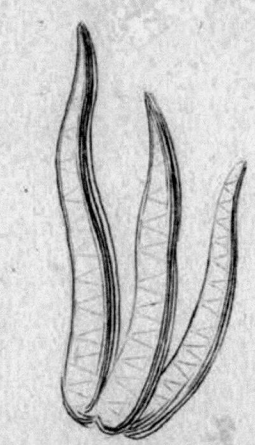

Portion de flamme du Manteau de l'Ordre du St Esprit qui présente la manière de guiper avec le clinquant.

a. Les parties unies doivent être exécutées en passé, des Paillétes dans l'intérieur.
b. Couchure. c. La pratique, petite chainette qui sert à coudre sur l'étoffe. d. Feuille en passé.

THE MISTRESS OF EMBROIDERY

PAGE 27

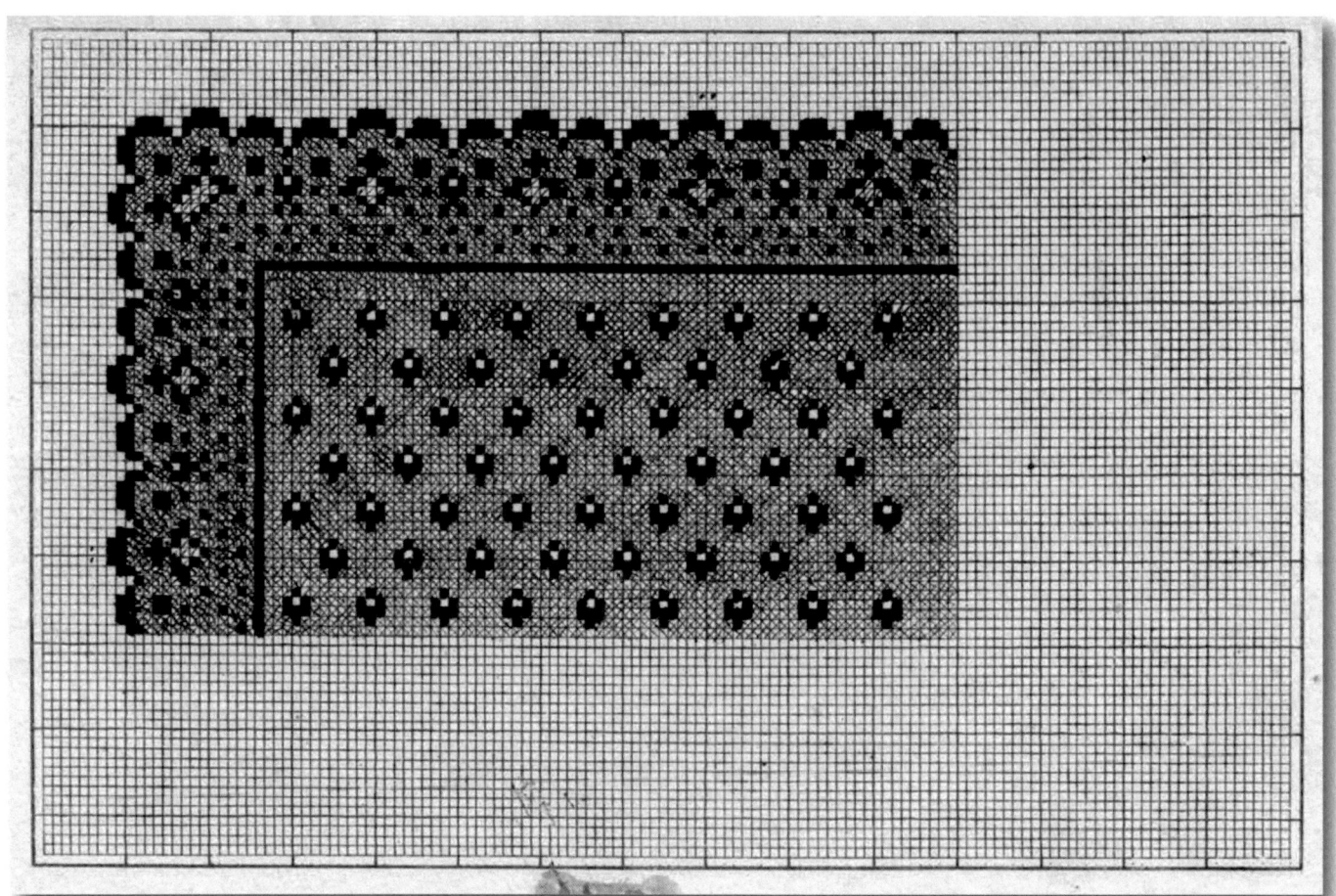

THE MISTRESS OF EMBROIDERY PAGE 28

═╫═ 1819 ═╫═

LA MAITRESSE DE BRODERIE
The Mistress of Embroidery

These patterns are reproduced from a portfolio of small plates in my private collection. They originally accompanied the book "La Maitresse de Broderie" published in 1819 by French artist Augustin Legrand.

Legrand's needlework designs were eventually purchased and published by Jacques Simon Sajou in his collections. Later editions showcased patterns in tiny, fold-out booklets sized for a lady's workbag or basket; charts were printed on a long strip of paper folded up into accordion-like pleats which led to the nickname "leporello."

These classic motifs, borders and scenes are easily adapted by modern needleworkers; designs charted on graph paper are a universal language to be translated into needlepoint, counted cross stitch and beadwork.

Made in the USA
Middletown, DE
12 December 2018